NOVEL BASICS

Tools To Transform Your Idea Into A Real Work Of Fiction

Elena L. Moore

NOVEL BASICS
Tools To Transform Your Idea Into A Real Work Of Fiction

ISBN-13: 978-1469903033
ISBN-10: 1469903032

This book is dedicated to those who were told they would never be able to write but never gave up. May your stories find their wings.

The information and tools provided in this workbook are intended to be used as basic guidelines for writing a novel. It is not all inclusive nor does it assert to guarantee completion of a novel or security of a publishing contract. Individual results will vary.

CONTENTS

Introduction

Welcome to **Novel Basics**! I know first-hand that the quest to become a novelist is exciting, but it can also be daunting. Whether you are writing to pursue a publishing contract or to fulfill a personal goal, the questions are all the same. Where do you start? How do you start? Are you qualified? These, among many others, spin round and round in your head, sometimes tempting you to tuck your tail and run screaming for the hills.

Be strong, my fellow writer! You are headed in the right direction by participating in this workshop. In order to be successful, you need to learn as much as you can about the craft and the industry. This will not only help you to grow, but in time, will allow you to relax about the technicalities and focus more on the art itself.

This interactive workshop is designed to help you understand some of the basic elements of successful novel writing. Whether you are toying around with an idea for your first novel or are already in the frustrating throes of your third or fourth manuscript revision, **Novel Basics** can help. This series offers vital tips on developing intriguing characters, plot structuring, finding the right voice for your work and much more. **Novel Basics** will also equip you with some essential tools to help you organize your thoughts and arrange your ideas into a real breathing novel.

Writing a novel is a wonderful experience. But it comes with its fair share of challenges and sacrifice. You must be passionate about what you are doing or it will never happen. Having a great idea for a book is only the beginning. Only discipline and hard work will cause you to produce an actual finished work. But in the end, you will be rewarded with an amazing accomplishment that you can be proud of for life.

I am pleased that you will allow me to help in this stage of your career and wish you all the best in your endeavors.

Sincerely,

General Novel Writing Steps

The five steps outlined below will take you from your initial novel idea to a finished first draft of your **Manuscript**. These are general steps which each contain their own set of cascading tasks. However, if you follow this order, you will find that you are more focused and better prepared for each subsequent step.

1. Write your premise and begin plotting

2. Research and further plot development

3. Draft your outline

4. Write the story

5. Edit the first draft of manuscript

Getting Started!

By far, one of the hardest things about writing a novel is getting started. The odds always seem to be stacked against you when you look at it. Here are some tips that will help to get you going:

1. **Be Prepared** – Keep a notebook, iPad, laptop, camera and/or recorder with you at all times. You never know when you will be inspired. It may not be convenient for you to actually write, but equip yourself so that you are able to capture and jot down new ideas or notes for stories already in progress.

2. **Do Your Homework** – Always do your research on your subject matter, settings, character flaws, etc. You will find that it's easier to write when you are more informed. The better your research, the better your story will be.

3. **Prepare Your Story Outline** – If the method of outlining works for you, take the time to make a loose outline of your story. It should at least include your premise, beginning and ending. Though it is possible that the beginning and ending will change, this will at least give you some direction to get the story moving.

4. **Finding Time to Write** – Set aside a structured time each day to write, even if it's only 30 minutes at first. If you don't make the time, it won't miraculously open up. This will also help you become more disciplined about your craft.

5. **Set Realistic Goals** – Every writer is different. On average, a good day is when you write between three and five pages. Some days will be less, but on great days, you can do more. There are several factors which can affect your production. You may even want to set a goal of one page per day until you find your stride. Think about it: even if you only write one page, you are one page closer to your goal than the day before.

6. **Location is Vital** – Finding a comfortable place that allows you to be at peace and your imagination to run free is key to successful novel writing. Your space should be free from outside distractions and look, smell, and feel serene to you. You may need to switch locations from time to time for stimulation.

<u>NOTES</u>

_____

_____

_____

_____

_____

_____

_____

_____

_____

_____

_____

_____

_____

_____

_____

_____

_____

_____

Your Story Idea/Premise

The story **Premise** is generally a one sentence synopsis of your novel. It will outline two important points: *What happened to whom?* and *What are they going to do about it?*

Protagonist + Problem + Goal = Premise

Think of some of your favorite books or movies and write a premise for them.

Title: _____

Title: _____

Title: _____

Title: _____

<u>NOTES</u>

_____

_____

_____

_____

_____

_____

_____

_____

_____

_____

_____

_____

_____

_____

_____

_____

_____

Plot and Structure

The **Plot** is the heart of your story. It is a series of connected events based on cause and effect that tells the overall story. The plot is the vehicle that moves the elements of your story along and takes us to "The End."

Your plot should have an absolute structure of beginning, middle and ending.

Beginning	**Middle**	**Ending**
1. _Introduce Characters_ 2. _Character Arc Begins_ 3. _Paint the Setting_ 4. _Set Up the Conflict_ 5. _Exposition_	1. _Obstacles_ 2. _Tensions_ 3. _Mini Crises_ 4. _Character Arc Stretched_ 5. _Climax (closer to end)_	1. _Climax Resolution_ 2. _Loose Ends Resolved_ 3. _Change in Character Arc_
Opening Scenes	**_Heart of the Story_**	**_Denouement_**

<u>NOTES</u>

Setting the Scene

The **Setting** sets the stage, tone and sometimes the mood of your story. Creating three-dimensional and vivid settings can really bring your story to life. It is your job as the writer to paint a picture for your reader with words that organically transport them to a specific place, time and environment.

Whenever you develop settings, you must answer the following three questions in detail:

1. When does the story take place?

The anwer should include descriptors such as: past, present, future, winter, spring summer, fall, month, day, year, morning, afternoon, evening, during the Civil War, etc.

2. Where does the story take place?

The anwer should include descriptors such as: country, city, state, town, planet, inside, outside, house, school, museum, spaceship, submarine, stadium, etc.

3. What are the conditions of the environment?

The answer should include descriptors such as: weather, sounds, noise, quiet, trees, light, dark, eerie, etc. It should also describe the other objects in the place (old spooky house, peeling paint, contemporary chair, etc.).

Setting is important throughout your story, not just in the beginning. The reader should be able to visualize where the characters are in every scene.

Novel Outline Worksheet

You can use this **Outline Worksheet** to build your story. It can help keep you on track to arrive at your desired ending. Remember, this outline is ***only a guide***. As your story develops, you may add, delete or change elements several times as you learn your characters better. It's a natural part of the process!

Working Title: _____

Premise:

This story is about...

Opening:

Chapter Events or Major Story Elements in Order of Occurrence *(Loose Plot)*:

1.	
2.	
3.	
4.	
5.	
6.	
7.	
8.	
9.	
10.	

Ending/Resolution *(Sometimes you know, sometimes you don't)*:

Character Profile Worksheet

You MUST create characters that are three-dimensional in order to draw your readers into the story. Use the worksheet below to help develop a ***Protagonist***.

Character's Full Name:		Nickname:	
Role:	Gender:		Age:
Occupation:		House/Apartment:	
Salary/Net Worth:		Car:	

Physical Characteristics:

Ethnicity:		Skin Tone:	
Body Style:		Hair (Color/Style):	
Height		Tattoos/Other Marks:	
Weight:		Eye Color:	
Face Shape:		Striking Features:	
Handicap:		Glasses/Contacts:	
Mannerisms:		Quirky Expressions:	

Emotional/Spiritual/Intellectual Profile:

Religion:		Optimist/Pessimist:	
Psychological Health:		Kind/Cruel:	
Introvert/Extrovert:		Trustworthy/Sneaky:	
Political Party:		Honest/Liar:	
Education:		Athletic/Lazy:	
Rational/ Irrational:		Strong/Weak:	
Habits:		Hobbies:	
Fears:			

Character Profile Worksheet *(Cont'd)*

Background *(Where from, childhood, etc.)*:

Secrets/Desires/Hardships, etc.:

Significant Relationships:

Spouse/Lover's Name:		Relationship Status:	
Child's Name:		Relationship Status:	
Friend's Name:		Relationship Status:	
		Relationship Status:	
		Relationship Status:	
		Relationship Status:	

Character Arc

A **Character Arc** is how the primary character(s) grow or change over the series of events that take place in a story. Characters begin the story with one viewpoint or attitude and through the events of the story, that viewpoint or attitude changes.

Generally only affects the main character in a story, though other characters can go through similar changes.

Basic Elements of a Character Arc:

Inciting Incident – The event that starts your protagonist's conflict or struggle and causes them to react.

Reaction – The character makes a choice due to an incident or action which affects the story's direction.

Action – External obstacle or consequence of character choice/reaction.

Climax – Point where the character is at his/her bottom or faced with their most intense obstacle. *ALWAYS* leads to another action/reaction.

Resolution – How the character uses information or new circumstances from the climax to resolve their problem.

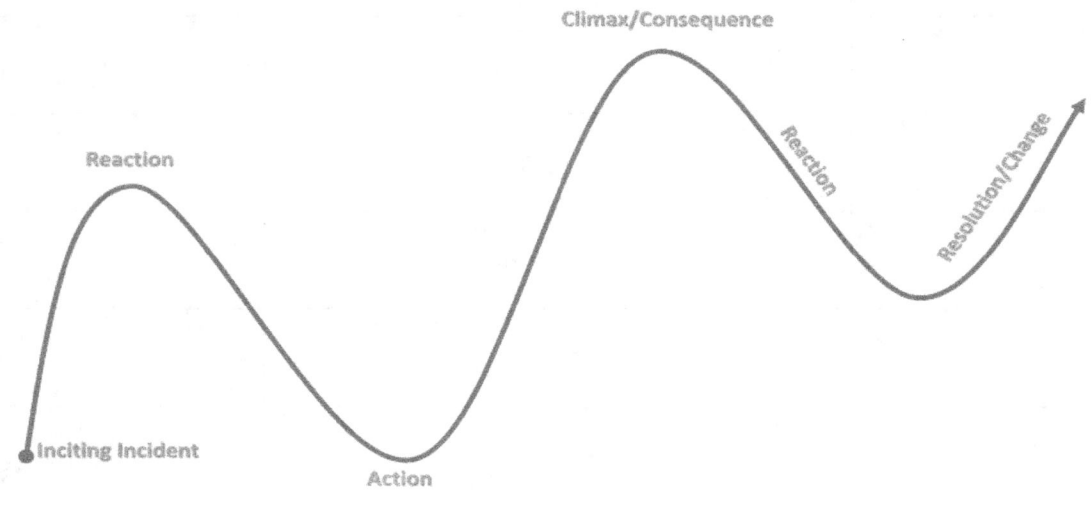

NOTES

_____

_____

_____

_____

_____

_____

_____

_____

_____

_____

_____

_____

_____

_____

_____

_____

_____

Narrative Perspectives

Narrative Perspective or *Point of View (POV)* is the viewpoint from which a story is told. There are five basic POVs used by authors as described below:

1. First Person POV

The story is told by a character who actually narrates the events from his or her perspective. They refer to themselves throughout the story as "I" or "we." This POV can be used to relay the thoughts and internal feelings of the narrator through a *Stream of Consciousness* to help add dimension to a character or give clues to the plot. Frequently, this POV comes from the protagonist, but not always.

> *Stream of Consciousness* is an internal monologue of the narrator that reveals his or her feelings and thought processes without having to use actions or dialogue.

2. Second Person POV

This viewpoint is used the least in literature. The narrator refers to characters as "you" as if you are a part of the story. This POV is most commonly used for preschool programs where a character will invite children to sing along, etc. It is also used more commonly in song lyrics.

Third Person POVs

In contrast, this is the most commonly used viewpoint in literature. The narrator is not a character, but is the vehicle to relay the actions of the characters. The characters are referred to as "he", "she", "they", etc., but never as "I" or "we." There are three types of third person narration: subjective/limited, objective and omniscient.

3. Third Person Objective is when the narrator tells a story from an objective point of view as though you are watching the story through the lens of a camera. Of course, the camera is an inanimate object, therefore has no opinion. This viewpoint relies heavily on the action and dialogue of the characters. The reader is not privy to the internal thoughts and feelings of the

---

characters unless expressed through a **Soliloquy**. This viewpoint is sometimes used with the incorporation of articles and other documents to help paint the story.

4. Third Person Subjective/Limited is different from the objective viewpoint in that, in addition to action and dialogue, the narrator will also expose the thoughts and feelings of a character (limited) or several characters (subjective).

5. Third Person Omniscient is by far the most commonly used perspective. From this viewpoint, the narrator knows and tells everything, including the thoughts and feelings of characters. *"The Lord of the Rings"* by J. R. R. Tolkien is a great example. **Universal Omniscient** goes a step farther because the narrator knows information that the characters don't even know. (e.g., "Little did they know, the bridge ahead was no longer there.")

Alternating Between POVs
Some authors will alternate between first and third person POVs but it is not common. The general rule of thumb for novels is to use a single POV. It makes it easier for the reader to follow and reduces the margin for error in your writing.

NOTES

_____

_____

_____

_____

_____

_____

_____

_____

_____

_____

_____

_____

_____

_____

_____

_____

_____

<u>NOTES</u>

Narrative Tense

Narrative tense determines whether you will write your story in past, present or future tense.

Past Tense

Past tense is used most commonly in literature. The story is depicted as to have occurred at some time prior to the present. The author will use past tense verbs to describe actions (e.g., "They ate.", "He slept.")

Present Tense

Present tense stories read as though the events are happening right now. The author will use present tense verbs to describe action (e.g. "She slowly opens the door.", "He is singing the song softly.")

Future Tense

Using future tense, story events are written almost prophetically as they will take place in the future. The author will almost always use the future tense helping verb "will" to describe actions. (e.g., "He will fall into a volcano.", " They will be rich.") Future tense is rarely used in novel writing.

<u>NOTES</u>

Writing Great Dialogue

Great Dialogue is vital to a successful novel. It is how the characters of your story carry out conversations. Dialogue serves three primary functions:

1. To move the story along;

2. To help with character development by providing information about the characters (personality, struggles, education, culture, etc.);

3. To provide details or other information about the story or past events that affect the story.

Basic Dialogue Rules to Remember:

1. Dialogue is always set in quotations.

2. Punctuation is always inside of closing quotation.

3. Start a new paragraph every time a new character speaks.

4. Identify who is speaking by use of attributions or dialogue tags *(he said, she asked, etc.)*.

5. Character dialogue does not have to be proper English or complete sentences.

6. Each character should have his/her own distinct way of speaking and remain true to that throughout the story.

7. Do not overuse dialogue tags.

<u>NOTES</u>

<u>Industry Manuscript Guidelines</u>

1. **Paper size:** 8.5" x 11"

2. **Margins:** 1" all around (top, bottom, left & right) – allows editors room for notes

3. **Font Type:** Courier, Courier New (preferred) or Times New Roman

4. **Font Size:** 12point

5. **Cover Page:**
   - **Top left corner:** Name, address, phone number and email (single-spaced, left-justified)
   - **Middle center:** Title, by and name (all double-spaced and centered)
   - **Top right corner:** Word count rounded to the nearest thousand across from your name)

6. **Running Header:** Should be right justified and include:
   Name/Title/Page number (not on cover page)

7. **Justification:** Left to leave ragged edge– never block justified!

8. **Bold and Italics**: Never use bold or italics – underline only.

9. **Indents:** Exactly .5" for new paragraphs – use the tab key, not space bar.

10. **Spacing:** Double spaced

11. **Dialogue:**
    - Always start a new person's dialogue on a new line
    - Use comma after a leading tag

12. **Chapters:**
    - Each chapter should have a chapter page. The title or chapter number should be one to six lines (double spaced) from the top and centered.
    - New chapters should ALWAYS start on a new page.

13. **End of Story Indicator:** Use "####" or "The End" on the last page to indicate the end of your story.

Useful Definitions

Antagonist: The adversary of the hero or protagonist in a story.

Arc: How the primary character(s) grow or change over the series of events that take place in a story. Characters begin the story with one viewpoint or attitude and through the events of the story, that viewpoint or attitude changes. A character arc generally only affects the main character in a story, though other characters can go through similar changes.

Climax: The moment of greatest intensity in the plot of a literary work, generally bringing events to a head and leading to the conclusion.

Denouement: *(dey-noo-mahn):* The final resolution of the intricacies of a plot, as of a drama or novel.

Exposition: Sets up the main plot for a story. It can also give depth to the characters and expound on their backgrounds.

Fiction: Literary works invented by the imagination.

Flat Character: A relatively uncomplicated character that does not go through character development over the course of the story.

Manuscript: The typed version of a literary work before it is published.

Non-fiction: Literary works that offers information, opinions or assumptions based on facts and reality, including biographies and history.

Novel: A fictitious narrative of considerable length and complexity, portraying characters and usually presenting a sequence of actions and scenes. The word count is on average between 80,000 and 100,000 words.

Novella: A fictitious narrative longer than a short story but shorter than a novel. The word count is generally between 17,000 and 40,000 words.

Useful Definitions (Cont'd)

Plot: Also called storyline, is a series of connected events based on cause and effect that tell an overall story.

POV (Point of View): Narrative Point of View is the viewpoint from which a story is told.

Premise/Logline: A one sentence synopsis of a novel. It outlines two important points: What happened to whom? and What are they going to do about it?

Protagonist: The leading character, hero, or heroine of a story.

Round Character: A character in fiction whose personality, background, motives, and other features are fully described by the author. These characters have fully developed and dynamic traits and undergo character development over the course of the story.

Setting: When and where a story takes place. It sets the stage, tone and sometimes the mood of the story.

Short Story: A short fictitious narrative, usually focused on one theme, and less than 10,000 words.

Soliloquy: Dialogue by a character who is talking to himself.

Stream of Consciousness: An internal monologue of the narrator that reveals his or her feelings and thought processes without using actions or dialogue.

Synopsis: A narrative summary of a work of fiction, generally 2 – 3 pages.

<u>NOTES</u>

NOTES

_____

_____

_____

_____

_____

_____

_____

_____

_____

_____

_____

_____

_____

_____

_____

_____

<u>NOTES</u>

NOTES

_____

_____

_____

_____

_____

_____

_____

_____

_____

_____

_____

_____

_____

_____

_____

www.ingramcontent.com/pod-product-compliance
Lightning Source LLC
Chambersburg PA
CBHW081801280526
45789CB00008B/2951